THINKING SKILLS

Challenging

Ready-to-go ideas and activities promoting
students' thinking skills across the curriculum.

Sharon Shapiro

Editor-in-Chief
Sharon Coan, M.S. Ed.

Art Director
CJae Froshay

Cover Artist
Lesley Plamer

Product Manager
Phil Garcia

Imaging
James Edward Grace

Publishers
Rachelle Cracchiolo, M.S. Ed.
Mary Dupuy Smith, M.S. Ed.

Blake Staff

Publisher
Sharon Dalgleish

Editor
Tricia Dearborn

Designed and illustrated by
Cliff Watt

Printed by
Printing Creations

INTRODUCTION

Today's students are the problem solvers of the future. However, in classrooms where teaching takes place at the level of factual knowledge only, the focus is on convergent thinking. Students learn to respond with conventionally correct answers rather than by exploring creative solutions.

All students can learn to think more critically and creatively. This book provides teachers with ideas and activities to help students develop these skills. The activities can be used to complement any classroom work in the various curriculum areas. They can be used in isolation, in sequence, or dipped into as teachers require.

In a future of guaranteed change, students will need to be adaptable. A grounding in creative thinking skills will enable them to pursue lifelong learning.

This edition published by

Teacher Created Materials, Inc.
6421 Industry Way
Westminster, CA 92683
www.teachercreated.com
©2001 Teacher Created Materials, Inc.
Made in U.S.A.
ISBN-0-7439-3625-6

with permission by

Blake Education
Locked Bag 2022
Glebe NSW 2037

CONTENTS

HOW TO USE THIS BOOK

TEACHERS' FILE

This section shows teachers how to make make the most of this book. It explains the reasons for strategies and suggestions for their use. It contains ideas for classroom organization as well as background notes, technology tips, assessment ideas, and suggestions for parent involvement.

QUICK STARTS

This section is written for teachers and includes activities, games, and ideas which will help teachers promote children's thinking skills. These activities can be used at any time, with little or no preparation, in any order, and incorporated across various curriculum areas to complement the regular classroom curriculum.

TAKE YOUR OWN TIME

This section contains 29 reproducible pages, covering topic areas such as Fluency, Flexibility, Categorizing, Questioning, Imaginative Visualization, Creative and Critical Thinking, and Originality. The pages can be used in any sequence and may also be modified and adapted to suit individual students or classes.

STEP BY STEP

This section contains task cards written for students. These can be used in activity centers for contract work at any time and in any sequence. Group and individual activities are included. They are aimed at students in the upper grades because of the reading required and the necessity for students to be able to follow instructions and complete the task independently.

TEACHER'S FILE

BACKGROUND NOTES

What is a thinking skill?

In addition to helping us think clearly, thinking skills help us critically and creatively collect information to effectively solve problems. As a result of learning thinking skills, students will also become more aware of decision-making processes.

Improved thinking encourages students to look at a variety of ideas, search to greater depth, practice more critical decision-making, challenge accepted ideas, approach tasks in decisive ways, and search for misunderstandings, while keeping the aims of the task clearly in mind.

The end results will be decisions that are more reliable, deeper understanding of concepts, contributions that are more creative, content that is examined more critically, and products that are more carefully crafted.

Why do students need to develop thinking skills?

Students need to develop the abilities to judge, analyze, and think critically in order to function in a democratic and technological society. A school as a whole should value the development of thinking skills and provide opportunities for these processes to be modeled and developed. Thinking skills can be taught, and all students can improve their thinking abilities. Creativity is present in all children regardless of age, race, socioeconomic status, and different learning modes.

The basic skills are generally considered to be reading, writing, and mathematics. These processes involve computation, recall of facts, and the basic mechanics of writing. Teachers should encourage mastery of basic skills as quickly as possible. Then avoid simply giving students more of the same work, as this merely creates boredom and frustration and reduces the children's opportunities to reach complex levels of understanding.

Unfortunately, research shows that too many teachers believe that if students calculate the correct answers to problems, they have learned thinking skills. Frequently students are faced with tasks that expect them to demonstrate their ability to use higher level thinking without having had the opportunities to develop their abilities with these thinking processes. The cognitive operations that make up thinking need to be explored, explained, taught, and practiced many times before they are mastered.

Some basic tips

Allow students to be nonconforming and encourage them to complete tasks in their own way. Encourage them to take risks, challenge ideas, and to reflect on tasks. If a child learns hundreds of facts but hasn't developed the ability to explore possibilities, much of the knowledge they gain will be wasted.

Thinking domains

It is desirable to develop different thinking domains, as they have different aims and develop different skills:
- *Critical thinking* examines, clarifies, and evaluates an idea, belief, or action's reasonableness. Students need to infer, generalize, take a point of view, hypothesize, and find temporary solutions.
- Brainstorming, linking ideas, using analogies, creating original ideas, organizing information, and looking at a problem from different perspectives will lead to alternative solutions useful in *decision making* and *problem solving*.
- The *collection*, *retention*, *recall*, and *use* of information when needed is another vital skill.
- *Creative thinking* aims for original ideas.

Thinking Processes

Eight processes, divisible into cognitive and affective abilities, have been identified as being important in fostering thinking skills:

Cognitive abilities
- *Fluency* is where as many ideas as possible are thought of by students.
- *Flexibility* is where students look at problems from different perspectives and think of ways to combine unusual ideas into something new and different. At times objects may have to be grouped according to different criteria.
- *Originality* involves producing unusual or unique ideas.
- *Elaboration* involves adding or further developing ideas.

Affective (feeling) abilities
- *Curiosity* involves working out an idea by instinctively following a pathway.
- *Complexity* involves thinking of more complex ways of approaching a task. This may involve searching for links, looking for missing sections, or restructuring ideas.
- *Risk-taking* is seen in students who guess and defend their ideas without fear that others will make fun of their thoughts.
- *Imaginative* students can picture and instinctively create what has never occurred, and imagine themselves in other times and places.

ASSESSMENT

Allow time for completion of activities and create opportunities for responses to be shared in a group. One way students learn is by mirroring the behavior and responses of others. As general rules:
- Do not grade activities but display them.
- Do not criticize students' responses or drawings.
- Find something to value whenever possible.

There needs to be continuity in the way students are assessed so that information is cumulative and accurate. Progressive files for the children should include information about their strengths, weaknesses, and any special achievements or creative results they have achieved.

Note carefully any changes or unusual results or progress, especially in highly creative areas such as story writing, art, special projects, research, inventions or music. Encourage students to examine and assess their own abilities and goals to obtain insight into themselves and the way they tackle a problem.

For a photocopiable sheet of fun awards for proficiency in thinking, see page 44.

The Classroom Environment

The learning environment should allow for creative expression, nurtured by questions, tasks, exploration, and play. Create flexible working and seating spaces so that students have greater freedom to move around to different areas of the classroom, depending on tasks they are completing. Develop areas for independent work, small-group work, and areas where the whole class can meet. Bring in carpet squares or mats, beanbags and pillows so students can work comfortably while sitting on the floor or working in groups.

Vary the shapes of areas and the color of different sections of the classroom to vary the mood and create interest. By including shapes such as hexagons, pentagons, spheres, and domes, scope is created to challenge students with numerous environmental problems. Colors can be used to set the mood for the type of work students will be doing in a vicinity. Red will stimulate thought and orange will energize the children, while yellow will vitalize and accelerate mental activities. Green and blue soothe and calm over-excited students and are ideal to incorporate in a quiet reading area.

Organize materials systematically so students have easy access to them. Use open shelving, boxes, cartons, wine bottle boxes, and ice cream buckets to store activities and resources.

Learning Centers

A thinking skills learning center can contain games and puzzles, relevant books, and a computer set up with a specific thinking skills program (such as the program *Thinkin' Things*, distributed by Edmark). Building materials such as Lego or Meccano can be used for constructing unusual devices. A book can be kept in which students can record discoveries or useful tips for students who will be working there in future.

Folders of worksheets can be added to as new ones are gathered. You can also keep a folder that students can contribute to, for example, by writing a question for other students to consider (What would you do if ...?) or making up a puzzle or adding in one they've found. (If the addition is a puzzle, the student should make sure the answer is included on the back of the page.) Towards the end of the year, these can be gathered into a booklet and a copy made for each student.

Aim for Diversity and Balance

Ensure that there is variety in the way students are working. Encourage them to work independently at times, in small groups, with older students, or as peer tutors.

Strive for a balance between structured and unstructured tasks and convergent and divergent tasks. Encourage students to use techniques that change from hands-on, to visual, oral, or written, so a variety of learning styles are used. At different times and for different tasks, it is best to discuss, dramatize, or work from contracts or at learning centers. This variety will help with active involvement, thinking skills, motivation, and longer periods of concentration.

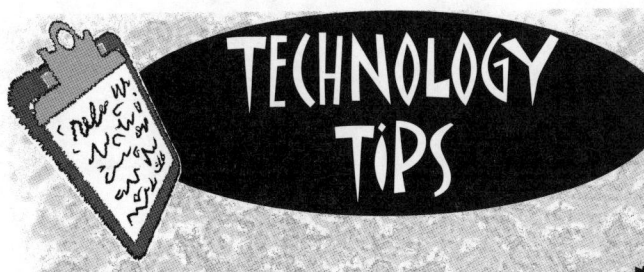

TECHNOLOGY TIPS

Computing skills can be integrated into many aspects of the learning experience. Computer technology is useful for programming and problem solving. LOGO language has been written with children in mind. Children can type in instructions to create individual designs and drawings. Spreadsheets and databases develop higher order skills and lateral thinking. They will also develop spatial orientation. A program called *Thinkin' Things*, containing age-appropriate activities, is available from Edmark.

Computer games can be used to motivate students and encourage task commitment. When software is carefully selected, it can be used to develop higher-order thinking skills. Simulation or strategy software is motivational and open-ended and involves players in critical thinking, risk-taking, and real-life problem solving.

Technology in the form of board games can be used to encourage and develop thinking skills. Students learn rules and apply different strategies in games such as chess, Abalone, and Scrabble.

PARENT INVOLVEMENT

Parents can be informed in a take-home note that students will be learning thinking skills. Emphasize the facts that children are the problem solvers of the future and that parents can encourage their development in this area. Learning thinking skills will enable children to deal with complex situations using a range of thinking strategies and will also equip them to learn throughout their lives.

On a purely practical level, parents' help can be enlisted in gathering unusual games and puzzles which can be located at a learning center in your classroom.

There are many questions that parents can ask of themselves: Do our children have opportunities to work on problems where creative thinking is valued? Are they given opportunities at home to write story endings differently? Are they encouraged to apply history's lessons to today's problems? Are they involved in planning family outings that will satisfy the needs of all family members? Are they allowed to participate in family projects such as redesigning rooms?

Most importantly, are children allowed to be different? Are they listened to, even if their ideas are unusual or impractical? Are they reassured that, even if they are disagreed with, their ideas and input are valuable? In terms of the family as a whole, are they encouraged to be part of an environment where it is acceptable to make mistakes and where the focus is on learning from them?

QUICK STARTS

Fairy Tales in Color

Read a number of fairy tales to the class, focusing on the use of different colors to create moods, characters, and images. Each color and its purpose should be listed and discussed. Ask students to suggest other fairy tales where the use of colors is important and discuss the reasons for this.

Population Explosion!

Tell the class that they should imagine that the world has become so crowded that people are struggling to find a place to live. Students should list all the ways that the problem could be overcome.

Six Words

Present six words to the class and ask students to write as many sentences as they can using these words. Can they write a sentence that includes all the words?

Brainstorm!

Have groups of students brainstorm these topics:
• Explain the emotions of a gate.
• Describe the different ways that warmth can be seen.
No answers are right or wrong, and the aim is quantity not quality. Have groups share their answers with the class so students can learn from others' thinking.

Lunch Box

Arrange students into small groups and ask them to think of different ways to finish the following sentence: This country is like a lunch box because .... After they have completed this task, have groups read their answers aloud, and discuss them as a class.

No Holidays!

Tell students to imagine that school holidays, which were due to begin tomorrow, have been cancelled. Students should invent and list twenty reasons why this may have happened. Students should then check the three reasons they think are the most creative and share them with the class.

Train Delay

Students should imagine that their train has been stopped for an unknown reason and that there will be a long delay. There are twelve other passengers in the carriage. Have students invent as many ways as possible to entertain themselves and the other passengers.

Umbrelon

Choose two unrelated objects, such as a melon and an umbrella, and ask students to combine them, choose a name for the new object, and then list what the qualities of the object are and what the object could be used for. Students could draw the new object. The drawings could be displayed around the classroom.

Down the Drain

Suggest to students that a new ball has rolled down a gutter and fallen into the storm drain. Have students discuss and list ways of retrieving the ball. Give students the following rules: they must not climb into the pipe, and the only objects available to use are a glove, a wheel, and one other item of their choice.

Square Eggs!

Ask students to visualize a square egg. Ask them to explain, in detail, how they think this egg could be used and what might be the advantages and disadvantages of its shape.

Rush Hour

Discuss the early morning and late afternoon rush hours in the city when buses are overcrowded. Group students and ask them to think of ways to modify the bus without enlarging it. The improved bus should allow more people to travel, and they should all be able to travel in greater comfort. Discuss the suggestions with the class.

Mouse House

Have students design a house for a mouse using craft sticks, rubber bands, and a napkin. Students should draw their designs and explain how they work. Designs can be displayed in the classroom.

Be Safe!

Have students list their ideas on how roads could be made safer for bicycles. Students could discuss experiences they have had while riding bicycles where they did not feel safe and ways these experiences could be avoided.

SCAMPER

SCAMPER is a tool that students can use to redesign an object.

S Can anything be *substituted*?
C Can ideas, events, or contents be *combined*?
A Can anything be *adapted*?
M Can anything be *modified*, *magnified*, or *minified*?
P Can the *purpose* be changed?
E Can anything be *eliminated*?
R Can the pace, order of events, and manner, be *reversed*?

Ask students to apply this strategy to redesigning a telephone.

BAR

B makes an object *bigger or smaller*.
A *adds* on to an object.
R *replaces*, *changes*, and/or *rearranges* an object.

BAR is useful for helping students focus on different facets of an object's design and can assist them when revising and redesigning objects for uses other than those for which they were originally intended. Ask students to use BAR to redesign a bicycle.

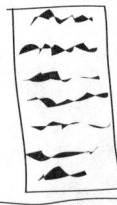

Which Article?

Select two newspaper articles giving accounts of the same event. Group students and have them study the articles and then discuss how the events are interpreted in each article. Are the events treated in a similar manner? If not, why do the students think this might be so?

Jelly legs!

Ask students to imagine that their bodies are made of jelly. They should then list everyday things that they would not be able to do and how their new bodies would affect their daily activities. What would they be able to do that they can't do with their current bodies?

Who's in the Zoo?

Have students list all the animals they have seen at the zoo. Then have them compare the advantages and disadvantages for animals of living in a zoo. Set aside time for students to ask any questions they may have about the animals (for example, how the animals are fed and exercised).

Books, Books, Books!

Have students list and classify the books that the class has read this year. To classify books, students can use important characteristics or attributes of characters, objects, places, or ideas. Discuss and compare the lists as a class.

Spell Check!

Ask students to make a list of the words that they misspell most frequently. Have students classify these words according to what might be possible reasons for misspelling them. Display charts with the correct spellings around the classroom.

Great Ideas!

List all the ways you can celebrate a holiday.

_____

_____

_____

_____

_____

_____

_____

Suggest different ways that children can amuse themselves when they feel bored.

_____

_____

_____

_____

_____

How many different reasons can you think of why you might not be able to close the front door?

_____

_____

_____

_____

_____

_____

Thinking skill: Fluency

What Can You Combine?

List all the attributes of a jellybean. Focus on and think about the feel, the taste, the color, and any other attributes you can think of.

_____

_____

_____

_____

Think about something on the end of a rope and list all its properties.

_____

_____

_____

_____

Link some of the attributes found in the two objects to create something new. Draw this newly created object and explain how it functions.

_____

_____

_____

_____

_____

Thinking skill: Fluency and flexibility

That's Criminal!

Work in groups of three. List all the crimes you can think of, for example, harming someone's property, theft, hurting a person, etc.

Rank the crimes from least serious to most serious and write at least three reasons for your answer. What should be the punishment for each crime?

List of crimes	Ranking	Reasons	Punishment

Thinking skill: Fluency and flexibility

18

Make a List

An athletic event has been postponed for four weeks. Brainstorm all possible reasons.

_____

_____

_____

_____

_____

_____

_____

List all the different ways that you can think of to greet people.

_____

_____

_____

_____

_____

_____

List as many uses as you can for a bucket.

_____

_____

_____

_____

_____

_____

List at least ten changes that could possibly occur if there were no television programs being transmitted.

_____

_____

_____

_____

_____

_____

_____

_____

_____

_____

_____

Thinking skill: Fluency and flexibility

Listing Change

Write a list of things that change rapidly and a second list of things that change slowly.

Rapid Change	**Slow Change**

Write a list of things that change daily, for example, world population.

List things that never change.

Thinking skill: Fluency and flexibility

Using Technology

Name all the machines that you could possibly use during an average day.

_____   _____

_____   _____

_____   _____

_____   _____

_____   _____

Imagine you were living in the 19th century and were suddenly transported to the present day. What do you imagine you would find most surprising?

_____

_____

_____

_____

_____

_____

_____

What do you think would be most frightening?

_____

_____

_____

What would be most amusing?

_____

_____

What could be most useful out of all the inventions in the 20th century?

_____

_____

Thinking skill: Fluency and flexibility

Curly Questions

The answer is "Fame."
List 5 questions.

1. _____
2. _____
3. _____
4. _____
5. _____

Choose a famous person. [   ]

If you could talk to that person, what would be 3 questions you'd ask and what do you think the answers might be?

_____
_____
_____
_____
_____
_____
_____
_____
_____
_____
_____
_____
_____

Thinking skill: Questioning

22

Asking Questions

There was a fire in the North Sounds neighborhood last night and, sadly, one family's house has burned down. The family has no access to money for a week and no food or shelter.

Brainstorm questions that you would like to ask the family about the scene and their current situation. Place an asterisk (*) next to the three questions that you believe are the most important.

_____

_____

_____

_____

_____

_____

_____

_____

_____

_____

_____

A person who has gone to the movies runs out of the theater screaming. Brainstorm questions that you would ask bystanders to find possible reasons for this.

_____

_____

_____

_____

_____

_____

_____

_____

Thinking skill: Questioning

What Rubbish!

Think of at least four different ways to clear paper, discarded food, and other trash from the parking lot of your local shopping center. Draw your solutions below.

Thinking skill: Originality

24

What Could This Be?

List two objects or images that each drawing could be.

I am an open mouth...

...or a rubber ball.

_____
_____

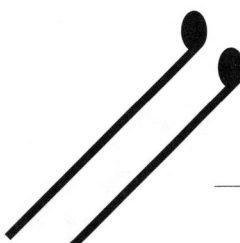
_____
_____

_____
_____

_____
_____

_____
_____

Draw one of your own and have a friend guess what it is.

_____
_____
_____
_____
_____

Thinking skill: Forced relationships

Clean the Graffiti

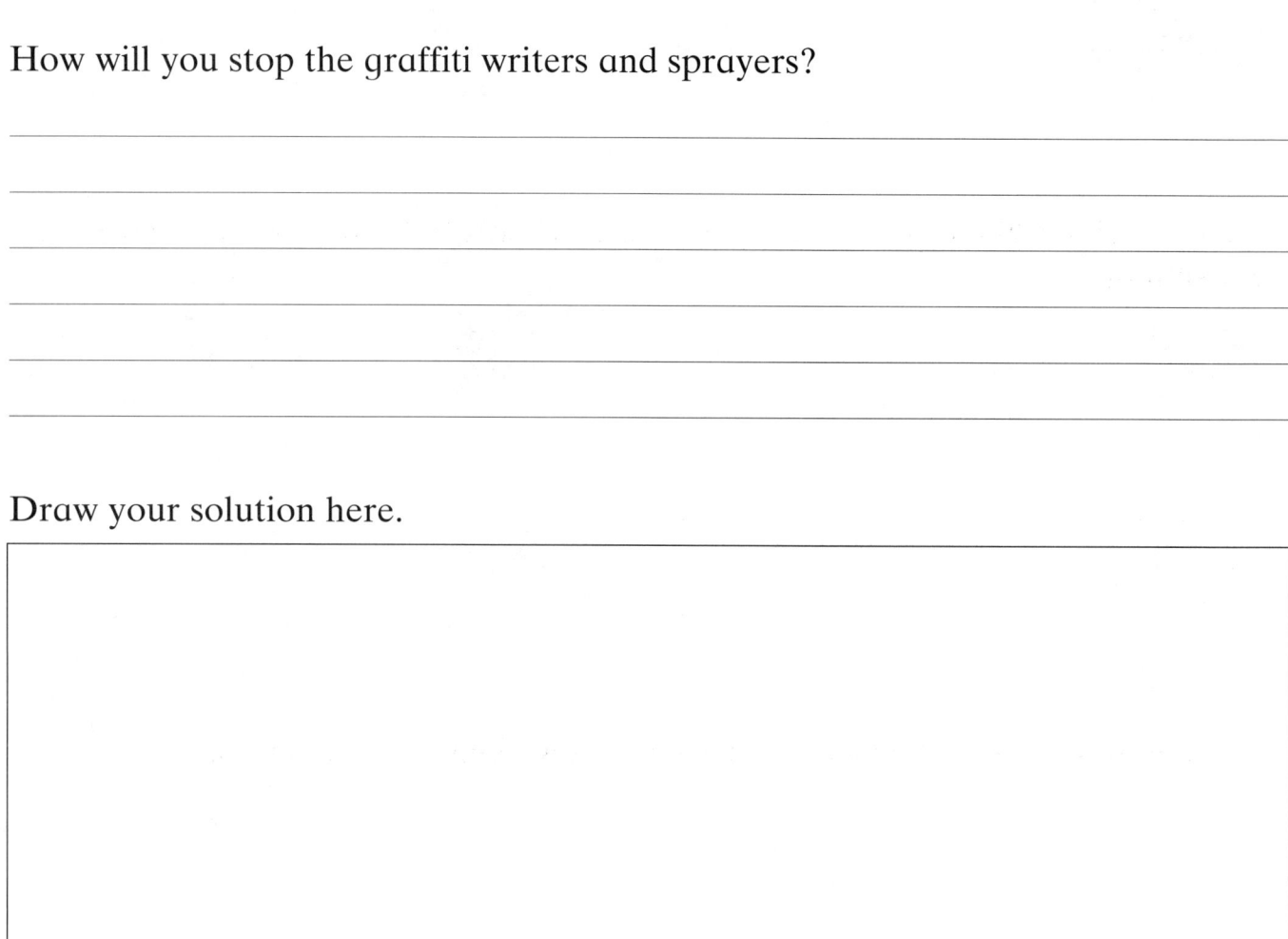

Your school has a terrible problem with graffiti. Think of ways that you can stop this from happening. Your solution must involve a human, something mechanical, and something that has to be eaten.

How will you stop the graffiti writers and sprayers?

_____

_____

_____

_____

_____

Draw your solution here.

Thinking skill: Forced relationships

Picture the Scene

Why is the airplane's arrival delayed? Think of at least five reasons.

_____

_____

_____

_____

_____

How is a cloud like a pillow? List at least eight attributes or characteristics that are similar.

_____

_____

_____

_____

_____

_____

_____

Imagine that all the clocks have stopped. How would this affect you?

_____

_____

_____

_____

_____

_____

_____

Thinking skill: Imaginative visualization

Come and Play

Imagine you are in a junkyard. There are old tires, ladders with missing rungs, empty paint cans, boxes, ropes, old cabinets, etc.

Think about how you might use these items to design a safe playground for a number of students. Think about what other recycled items you would like to add for further activities. Write your ideas here.

_____

_____

_____

_____

_____

_____

Draw a map of your new playground in the space below, labeling its different items.

Thinking skills: Imaginative visualization, originality, elaboration

Land With No Gravity

Work in groups of three. Focus on an imaginary land where there is no gravity. Picture the people, colors, shapes, sounds, and smells. Picture the homes, landscape, buildings, traffic, etc.

What are the people doing? Where are they going?

Have one group member draw while the other two describe the scene with their eyes shut. The drawer can add details as long as they fit with the image. It is a good idea to complete a rough drawing before completing a final copy here to ensure that you include all the details.

Thinking skill: Imaginative visualization

Be Creative

Design a device that will save time by doing something that is normally done manually (by hand). Explain how it will work.

Drawing of device

Detailed explanation of how the device will work

_____

_____

_____

_____

_____

_____

Thinking skill: Creative thinking

Brushing Plus...

Crushing mechanism so more garbage fits.

Telescopic hands reach for garbage and put it in.

Water jets clean down surrounding area

Create an improved toothbrush. Ensure that for each change that is made, there is a clear explanation. You could use the BAR strategy to help you consider how different features could be improved.

B = make **bigger** or **smaller.**
A = **add** something.
R = **remove** something and **replace** it with something else.

Thinking skill: Creative thinking

Redesigning a Tricycle

Choose five unconnected words.
Check their meanings in a dictionary.

Word   Dictionary meaning

1. _____   _____

2. _____   _____

3. _____   _____

4. _____   _____

5. _____   _____

Now, draw and explain how you would use the five words to make changes to the tricycle. (For example, if you chose the word *elastic*, you might want to design an elastic tricycle that shrinks so it's easy to step onto and then recovers its normal size so you can ride it easily.)

Thinking skill: Creative thinking

New Products

Brainstorm ideas for each list.

Different types of clothing,
for example, shoes

_____

_____

_____

_____

_____

Different modes of transport,
for example, train

_____

_____

_____

_____

_____

With your eyes closed, select one object from each list. Combine them to
form a new object. Sketch and name the new object.

How would this new product affect
your life? Describe what it could do.

_____

_____

_____

_____

_____

_____

_____

_____

Thinking skill: Creative thinking

NAME

The Amazing Hat!

Design a hat that has four uses. Draw it here
and label all its parts.

Describe how it works and who it would be useful for.

_____

_____

_____

_____

_____

_____

_____

_____

_____

_____

Thinking skill: Creative thinking

New, Improved...!!!

Design a new shower, and explain the reasons for any changes. You may want to use the BAR strategy to help decide on features that could be improved and ways of doing it. Illustrate your new shower design below.

B = make **bigger** or **smaller.**
A = **add** something.
R = **remove** something and **replace** it with something else.

Change: _____

Reasons: _____

_____

Change: _____

Reasons: _____

_____

Change: _____

Reasons: _____

_____

Before...

After!

Thinking skill: Creative thinking

List the Attributes

Think of at least five attributes that a swing and vacuum have that are similar.

_____

_____

_____

_____

_____

_____

List and then combine some of the attributes of a child and water to create something new. Draw and describe it below.

Attributes of a child	Attributes of water
_____	_____
_____	_____
_____	_____
_____	_____

New object	Description
	_____
	_____
	_____
	_____
	_____

Thinking skill: Critical thinking

What a Legend!

Describe a hero or heroine who is living at the present time. Start with a physical description and then move beyond this to explain other qualities. Think of twelve heroic tasks that she or he might complete.

Description of hero or heroine	Explain the twelve heroic tasks.
	1.
	2.
	3.
	4.
	5.
	6.
	7.
	8.
	9.
	10.
	11.
	12.

You, as the hero, have to select three of the following objects to help with the tasks. Which would you choose and why would you choose them?

Choice   Reasons

_____   _____

_____   _____

_____   _____

> matches, jellybeans, a deck of cards, a rope, a skateboard, a magnifying glass, newspaper, a hat, a blanket, a boat, bicycle, a hammer, nails, money, shoes, soap, spoon, mirror, pocket knife, screwdriver, spade

Thinking skill: Critical thinking

Coping with Summer Hazards

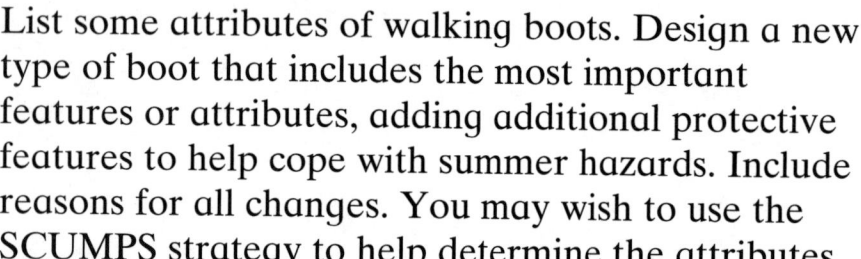

Walking in the forest or mountains can be treacherous, particularly during the summer months.

List some attributes of walking boots. Design a new type of boot that includes the most important features or attributes, adding additional protective features to help cope with summer hazards. Include reasons for all changes. You may wish to use the SCUMPS strategy to help determine the attributes.

S = size
C = color
U = use
M = materials
P = parts
S = shape

Attributes of walking boots

_____

_____

_____

_____

Your new design

Thinking skill: Categorizing

Out in Space ...

Work in groups of three. List as many objects as you can think of that you would find in outer space. Think of ways to group or categorize the objects, and give each category or group a label.

List

_____

_____

_____

_____

_____

_____

_____

Items listed under their categories

_____

_____

_____

_____

_____

_____

_____

_____

_____

_____

_____

Thinking skill: Categorizing

Look for a Pattern

bind, fasten, tighten — words to secure things

swim, jump, run, jog — different ways of moving

Work in groups of two or three. List thirty words, drawing them from newspaper articles, magazines, a chapter in a textbook etc. They should be varied and not follow one topic.

Word list	Divide the words into groups and describe each group.

Thinking skill: Categorizing

Reversing

?taht wonk uoy diD

It has been recorded that Leonardo da Vinci wrote his notes and observations backwards. Why do you think he did this?

_____

_____

_____

How do you think he was able to refer to them?

_____

_____

_____

Think about activities in your daily life. What would you like to reverse? How would you benefit?

Reverse	Benefit

Have someone tell you a message, then write it down backwards.

_____

_____

Can you read back what you have written? How did writing backwards make you feel?

_____

_____

_____

Thinking skill: Interpreting and inferring

Looking at All Sides

An animal walking across a busy road has been hit by a passing car. Should you help the animal?

Positives	Negatives	Questions you might have
_____	_____	_____
_____	_____	_____
_____	_____	_____
_____	_____	_____
_____	_____	_____

Summarize by explaining the consequences, potential dangers, and problems.

_____

_____

You dislike most of the lunch in your lunch box every day. Should you empty your lunch box into the garbage can at school each day?

Positives	Negatives	Questions you might have
_____	_____	_____
_____	_____	_____
_____	_____	_____
_____	_____	_____

What decision have you reached?

_____

_____

Thinking skill: Evaluation

Stamp Out Poverty

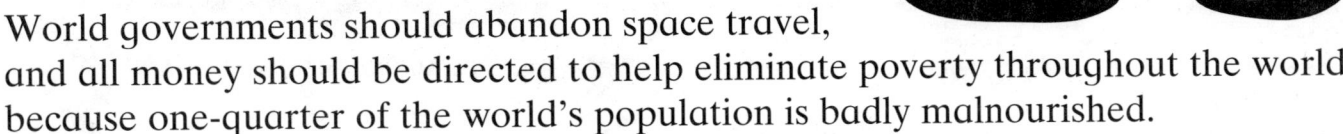

World governments should abandon space travel, and all money should be directed to help eliminate poverty throughout the world because one-quarter of the world's population is badly malnourished.

Examine the statement. List the positive and negative arguments and any questions that arise.

Positives	Negatives	Questions

What decision did you reach? Do you support the statement?

_____

_____

_____

Thinking skill: Evaluation

Thinking Skills Awards

Awarded to

_____

Fearlessly flexible!

Signed

_____

Date

_____

Awarded to

_____

Intrepid
interpreting!

Signed _____

Date _____

Awarded to

_____

**Thinking skills
wiz!**

Signed _____

Date _____

Awarded to

_____

for original thinking!

Signed _____

Date _____

STEP BY STEP

Skill: Evaluation

Examining an Issue

What you need:

- a newspaper
- pens
- paper

What to do:

1. Work in a group of three.
2. Find an article about a controversial topic. In your group decide on a statement that summarizes one side of the controversy (for example, "There should be no oil drilling in Alaska").
3. Have one group member read the article aloud while the rest of you take notes under the three headings "Positives," "Negatives," and "Questions that Arise."
4. Discuss the notes. Did each notetaker see the same positives and negatives?
5. Discuss the issue, referring to your notes. Did your group come to an agreement on the issue or agree to disagree?
6. Now choose an issue relevant to school (for example, "Junk food should be available in the cafeteria" or "Students should wear uniforms to school.") and use the same procedure to evaluate and discuss it.

Skills: Critical and creative thinking

An Unusual Animal

What you need:

- drawing paper
- pencil
- eraser
- ruler

What to do:

1. Create an animal and make up a name for it.
2. Describe its appearance, habitat, the food it eats, its enemies, how it keeps itself happy and entertained, and any special features. Draw its footprints. Construct or draw its body and natural habitat.
3. This animal is threatened with extinction. Develop a campaign that will publicize the threat and help save your animal.
4. Your animal is being transported to a zoo. Design a perfect enclosure, thinking about its natural environment and what its needs are.

News Item

What you need:

- drawing paper
- pencil
- eraser
- ruler

What to do:

1. Visualize the following scene: Engine-driven vehicles have been banned because the pollution is affecting the entire community. The only acceptable means of transportion are skateboards and bicycles.

2. Brainstorm the ways the change in transportion would affect traffic control, clothing manufacturers, gasoline sales, supermarkets, and medical care.

3. Develop new road rules for your community. List them so they can be circulated to road users. Ensure that all rules are clarified by appropriate drawings.

Don't Get Wet!

What you need:

- drawing paper
- pencil
- eraser
- ruler
- sticks
- rubber bands
- string

What to do:

You have dropped your watch into a fish pond! How will you get it out without getting your hands wet or hurting the fish?

1. Design a device that can be used to do this. Incorporate a stick, rubber bands, and a piece of string. (You can add other objects if you need to.)

2. Now construct your device to test its efficiency.

Enjoy Your Lunch

What you need:

- a shoebox
- odds and ends
- paper
- pen

What to do:

1. You want to determine the positives and negatives of the design of a standard lunch box. Develop a questionnaire to survey students.

2. Conduct the survey.

3. Prepare a summary of the findings and decide which aspects can be incorporated into a new design for the lunch box. It is important not to lose the positive aspects in your redesign!

4. Draw your new design, explaining the reason for each change.

5. Use a shoebox to construct a prototype of your new design.

A New Sport

What you need:

- drawing paper
- pencil
- eraser
- ruler
- cardboard
- scissors

What to do:

1. List all the attributes you can think of for tennis, music, and basketball.

2. Design a new sport for students your age, using a combination of the attributes you listed.

3. Develop a set of rules and design an area for the game to be played on or in. (It might be a court with markings or perhaps it would be better suited to an orchestra pit.)

4. Design an advertising campaign to popularize your new sport. What will be its selling points — that it's completely stupid and good fun or a challenging game that improves fitness and co-ordination ... ?